THE GREEK POINT OF VIEW

THE GREEK
POINT OF VIEW

BY

MAURICE HUTTON

PRINCIPAL OF UNIVERSITY COLLEGE, TORONTO, AND PROFESSOR OF
GREEK.   SOMETIME SCHOLAR OF WORCESTER COLLEGE
AND FELLOW OF MERTON COLLEGE, OXFORD

NEW **GDH** YORK
GEORGE H. DORAN COMPANY

Made and Printed in Great Britain. Butler & Tanner Ltd., *Frome and London*

PREFACE

THESE chapters were begun several years ago and interrupted by sickness and other realities of life. When the sickness ended and took away part of the sunshine of life with it, I had leisure to return to the moonlight mists and mirages of literature, where values are distorted and often transposed; for —as my colleague, Professor W. J. Alexander, has said—the painful student who has laboured at the art of expression for a life-time has nothing to express; the man who has a life and a story to tell has never acquired the art of expression.

CONTENTS

CHAPTER I

THE GREEK CITY-STATE

IT is an idea of Plato's, in whom are anticipated all the ideas dominant or dormant in our own civilization, that a nation's character and happiness alike depend upon its form of government.

Aristocracy, according to Plato, must be the best form of political society, because in the realm of morals, aristocracy—the hierarchical organization of human qualities and instincts, the system which sets one quality and instinct above and another beneath, which gives to one a high and to another a humble place in one's life and actions, which repudiates passionately the equality of different qualities and different instincts—must be the principle of an honest man's private life (*Republic*, Book VII).

Democracy for the same reason, he thinks, must be a false political system, because, implying the equality of men, it implies also the equality of instincts and of qualities; the democrat is not merely the man who says that, for purposes of government, one man is as good as another; that is merely the superficial and political side of the mistake which he makes; he says that one instinct and one quality is as good as another; that a man's inner mind, the constitution in his heart, should be democratic, and should recognize every human quality and instinct as equally right and sound and entitled to equal expression; the political democrat, that is, passes, with Plato, into the moral democrat; and the true democrat is not the democratic politician but the democratic man; the man who resents the

tyranny of an inner law, not less than of the law
outside him ; who demands equality for his instincts
not less than, but far more than, equality for his
vote (*Republic*, VII). The French Revolution with
its French and Greek logic often illustrates Plato's
picture ; in that great Revolution everything which
suggested subordination, constraint, repression, co-
ercion, discipline and obedience, became suspect as
" royaliste " ; as aristocratic ; Madame Roland at
a very early stage of the Revolution, before she had
herself given occasion for scandal, complained that
decency and modesty had become " royaliste " in
the eyes of her Republican friends ; and Louvet,
one of the heroes of her Gironde, who ultimately
faced death bravely for the Girondist cause, himself
gave point and illustration to her complaints by his
earlier writings. The Revolution, in short, was not
against Louis only but against God : " Ni Dieu ni
maître " became its cry : as in Russia to-day since
the Great War.

To return to Plato : all travellers on ocean steamers
probably have at some time or other heard echoes
of the Platonic doctrine ; have listened with sym-
pathy or with distrust or even with disgust, according
to their temperament and their politics, to the naïve
and exuberant comments which the sight of the shores
of the United States awakes in the simple souls who
have sojourned long in European lands, and in the
presence of a society where classes are still some-
what sharply distinguished, and where that most
dubious of all European institutions, hereditary titles,
still remains.

" There is God's land," cries the simple soul which
has suffered, or imagines that it has suffered, from
hereditary aristocracy, while it plied in Europe
some humble trade, of digging drains, it may be, or
of herding swine. " There is God's land " ; because
here is political equality, and with political equality
happiness and self-respect, position and character.

An easy illustration of the prevalence of these
ideas is furnished by the reputation of " Walt
Whitman " (most characteristically so called). It
might have been assumed that these ideas alone,
without the aid of a literary sense, without more
charm of style than is implied in the selection of the
term " barbaric yawp " for his own writings, would
never have raised a man to eminence in literature :
yet the young " intellectuals " of the England of
those days built an altar for Walt Whitman out of
the matter and meaning of his work, regardless of
its form : and at the same altar the young intellectuals of England even still not unfrequently offer
incense : and on his own continent also there is
and has been ever since a cult of the poet so called,
embracing, if not the best American writers, at least
some good writers and some very interesting and
able men like Dr. Bucke.

And yet in spite of Plato and the French Revolution and the enthusiastic immigrant who comes
to the United States or to Canada to find a true
society for the first time, it probably will occur
both to the student of history and to the man educated
in Christian doctrine, that the connection between
political systems on the one hand, and happiness
or character on the other hand is slight, much
slighter than Plato or Walt Whitman (I apologize
to the shade of Plato for coupling his name with the
most frothy and superficial of the bellmen of
democracy) would have us suppose.

It is not merely the out-of-date Bull of a forgotten
Pope—

" How small of all the ills that men endure
The part that kings or laws can cause or cure "—

that suggests the historian's doubts ; it is also
—as already suggested—the strong bias of that
Christian education which still influences, if in a
lesser degree than formerly, the thought of our

times : if Christianity has brushed aside anything as unimportant, it has brushed aside the distinctions of political societies ; slowly, imperceptibly, indirectly by its spirit it has leavened all societies, until the subjection of women in the Oriental sense and the existence of slavery have become impossible, and even war itself has been rendered more humane and less frequent, in spite of the professional soldier and the professional pacifist, and in spite, too, of the new horrors of " the Great War " and the new atrocities of military science.

And yet Christianity has not directly attacked any political system ; it has always implied that these things are of the surface of life, and that nothing on the surface should count for much with the Christian. St. Paul—to quote the stock example—sent back Onesimus to his master to be a good slave again, and Nathaniel Hawthorne, twenty centuries almost after St. Paul, still had enough of the spirit of St. Paul in him to look with indifference at the crusade of his Abolitionist friends ; arguing that no political abolition could make the slave truly free, and no legal slavery could truly enslave him.

The argument, it is true, is unconvincing ; most of us, whether we still read Homer or not, are prepared to believe that the first step towards making a man respect himself is to make others respect him :

" Half of his worth doth the Father in Heaven who speaketh in thunder
Take from a man when the day of captivity cometh upon him."
(Homer's *Odyssey*, XVII, 392, 393. Cotterill's translation.)

" Drunk as a lord " has its parallel in the Greek vernacular ; but the parallel ran in Greece " Drunk as a helot " ; and we are aware also that the present enforcement of the death penalty by the State for murder only—once enforced for sheep-stealing—has done more than sermons or Christian doctrine to